LAUGH YOUR SOCKS OFF!

WORLD'S BEST (AND WORST) SPOOKY JOKES

EMMA CARLSON BERNE

Lerner Publications ◆ Minneapolis
>>>>>>>>>>>>>>>>>>>>

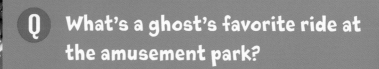

Q What's a ghost's favorite ride at the amusement park?

A The roller ghost-er.

Lerner Publications Company
A division of Lerner Publishing Group, Inc.
241 First Avenue North
Minneapolis, MN 55401 USA

For reading levels and more information, look up this title at www.lernerbooks.com.

Main body text set in Billy Infant Regular.
Typeface provided by SparkyType.

Library of Congress Cataloging-in-Publication Data

Names: Berne, Emma Carlson, author.
Title: World's best (and worst) spooky jokes / Emma Carlson Berne.
Description: Minneapolis : Lerner Publications, [2018] | Series: Laugh your socks off!
Identifiers: LCCN 2017035404 (print) | LCCN 2017016644 (ebook) | ISBN 9781512483581 (eb pdf) | ISBN 9781512483529 (lb : alk. paper) | ISBN 9781541511781 (pb : alk. paper)
Subjects: LCSH: Ghosts—Juvenile humor. | Monsters—Juvenile humor. | Riddles, Juvenile. | Wit and humor, Juvenile.
Classification: LCC PN6231.G45 (print) | LCC PN6231.G45 B47 2017 (ebook) | DDC 818/.602—dc23

LC record available at https://lccn.loc.gov/2017035404

Manufactured in the United States of America
1-43350-33170-8/10/2017

Q Why do ghosts love summer?

A It's boo-berry picking season.

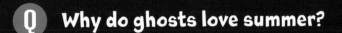
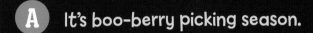

Q Why did the sad ghost love to go on airplane rides?

A They really lifted his spirits.

Q How did the ghost patch his sheet?

A With a pumpkin patch.

Q What is an eye doctor's favorite Halloween treat?

A Candy corneas.

Q What's it called when you get a skinned knee on Halloween?

A A boo-boo.

Q What do birds say on Halloween?

A Twick or tweet!

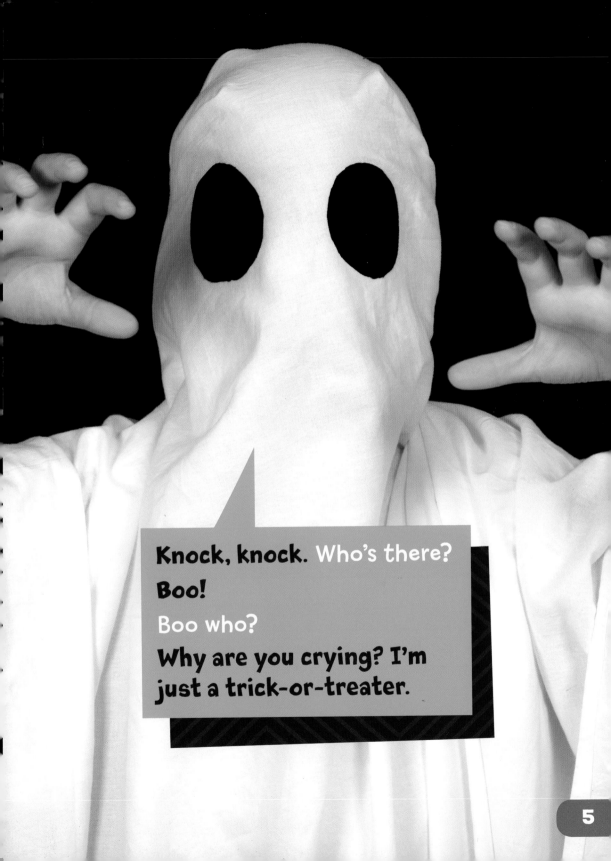

Knock, knock. Who's there?
Boo!
Boo who?
Why are you crying? I'm just a trick-or-treater.

Q What do you get when you cross a weeping willow with a UFO?

A A crying saucer.

Alien Chris: I have a surprise for you.

Alien Samantha: What is it?

Alien Chris: Close your eye first.

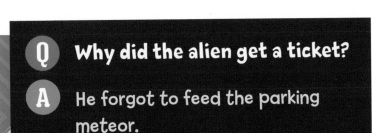

Q Why did the alien get a ticket?

A He forgot to feed the parking meteor.

HA! HA!

KNEE-SLAPPER

Q What did the alien say when his UFO landed in a backyard full of cats?

A Felines, take me to your litter!

7

Q Why didn't the witch fly on her broom when she was angry?

A She was afraid she'd fly off the handle.

A police officer was talking to a man who'd had his wallet stolen by a witch.

Here's the lineup, said the officer. Do you recognize the one who stole your wallet?

I'm not sure, Officer, the man replied. It's hard to tell which witch is which.

Q How do you make a witch itch?

A Just take away the w.

GROANER AWARD

Q Why do witches like hotels?

A They have broom service.

Q Why couldn't the mummy stop looking in the mirror?

A He was just too wrapped up in himself.

Q Why don't mummies go on vacation?

A They don't want to unwind.

Q What's a mummy's favorite music to dance to?

A Ragtime.

HA! HA!

Q Why couldn't the mummy wait to go to the music store?

A There was a sale on wrap music.

Q What do you get when you cross a snowman with a vampire?

A Frostbite.

Q Where do vampires keep their money?

A In a blood bank.

Q What do you call a glowing monster that sucks blood?

A A lamp-ire.

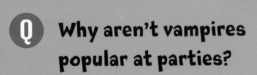

Q Why aren't vampires popular at parties?

A They're a pain in the neck.

GROANER AWARD

Knock, knock. Who's there?
Ivan.
Ivan who?
Ivan to suck your blood.

Knock, knock. Who's there?
Howl.
Howl who?
Howl I know you're not a werewolf?

Q Do monsters eat chips with their fingers?

A No. They prefer to have the fingers separately.

Q What monster loves to play tricks?

A Prank-enstein.

>>>>>>>>>>>>>>>>>>>>>>>>>>

Q What do man-eating monsters call their neighbors?

A Breakfast, Lunch, and Dinner.

<<<<<<<<<<<<<<<<<<<<<<<<<

Q Where do monsters like to go on vacation?

A Lake Eerie.

KNEE-SLAPPER

Mom! cried little Warren one morning. I don't want to go to school! Everyone says I look like a werewolf.

That's silly, his mother replied. Now go eat your breakfast and comb your face.

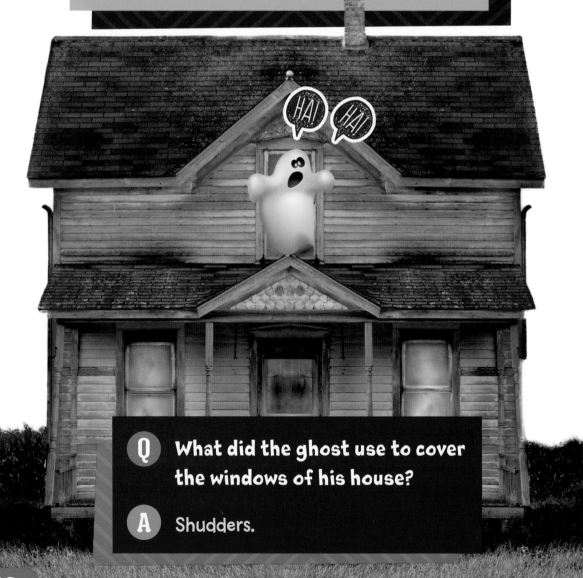

Q Why didn't the man buy the old mansion, even after the seller promised it wasn't haunted?

A The seller was a ghost, and the man could see right through him.

Q What did the ghost use to cover the windows of his house?

A Shudders.

Q How do ghosts open the door to their house?

A With a skeleton key.

GROANER AWARD

Q Why was the skeleton afraid to cross the road?

A He had no guts.

Q Why is the cemetery such a popular place?

A I don't know, but people are dying to get in.

Q Why did the doctor bring medicine to the graveyard?

A There was just so much coffin.

Q Why did the author go to the cemetery to write?

A He was looking for a good plot.

Q Why are cemeteries such serious places?

A They're full of grave stones.

Q What's a bat's favorite game?

A Bat-minton.

HA! HA!

KNEE-SLAPPER

Peee-you! said the bat to his brother.
You really need some mouthwash.
Why? asked his brother.
Can't you smell it? You have bat breath!

Q What exercise do bats do at night?

A Aerobatics.

Q What do you call a broomstick who's afraid of the dark?

A Petrified wood.

Q What are pirates afraid of?

A The darrrrrk!

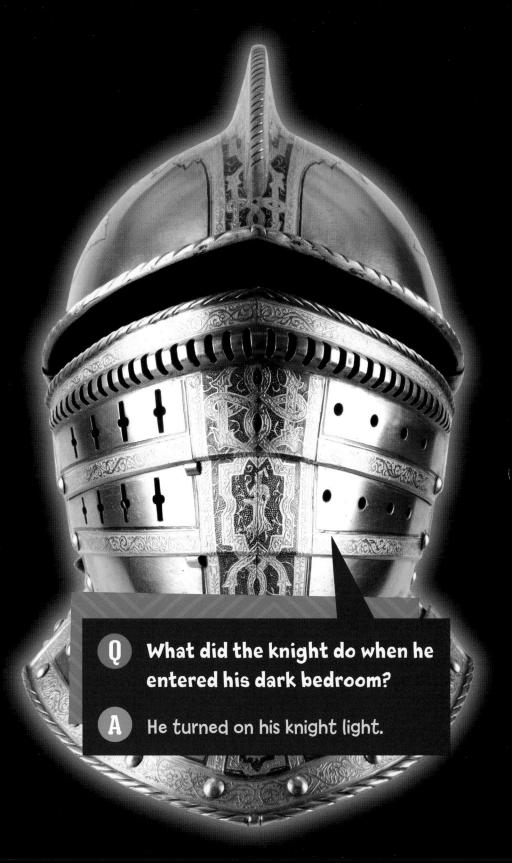

Q What did the knight do when he entered his dark bedroom?

A He turned on his knight light.

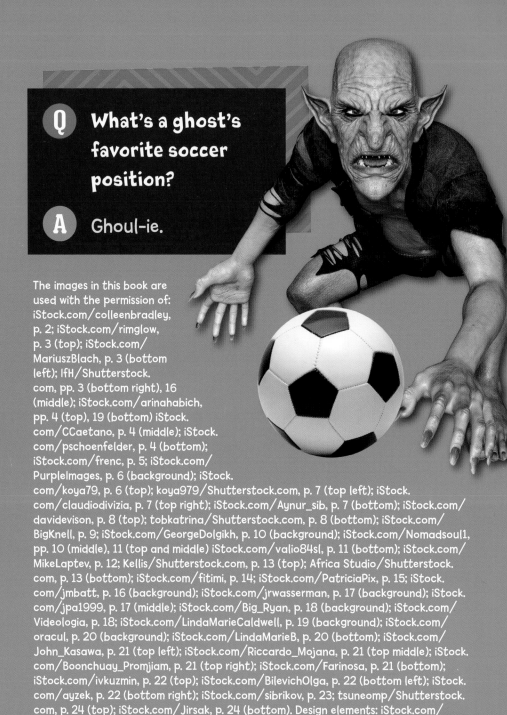

Q What's a ghost's favorite soccer position?

A Ghoul-ie.

24